Dedication

"Be thou exalted O God, above the heavens: and thy glory above all the earth." (Psalms 108:5)

This book is inspired by God and is written to glorify Him. May all who read this book feel the presence of the Holy Spirit as you read. May God richly bless and keep you until the day of Christ's return.

I would also like to thank God for my daughters, Lori Michelle and Rachel Elizabeth, my son-in-law Andrew, and my precious grandchildren, Conner Matthew and Kate Elise. They are all living proof of Matthew 21:22 which tells us "And whatever things you ask in prayer, believing, you will receive."

Glory to God, now and forevermore!

Evelyn Beelaert

Author's Preface

Dear Reader,

The book you have in your hands is a collection of spiritual events that have taken place during my lifetime, starting in 1987 when I was thirty-two to current day.

"Prayer Alerts" is specifically about the times the Holy Spirit has called me to pray urgently and then revealed to me afterward why I needed to pray. By combining all of these prayer alerts in a book I am sharing what God has done for me through the years. His love and watchfulness over our lives is amazing!

"Testimonies of Hope" were written originally to give to the homeless, to help them see God more clearly and to encourage them to come to know Jesus as their Savior and Lord. I have the honor of helping the homeless in Knoxville, Tennessee, along with Lost Sheep Ministries. God has put it on my heart to include these testimonies in this book and I hope they will inspire you as well.

"God Moments" are short stories that I hope you will enjoy. These stories are taken from times in my life that God answered my prayers or prayers of my friends in a surprising way. Praise His holy name!

I pray this book will renew your mind and that it will feed your spirit. I also pray you will be greatly blessed by all you read within these pages. I have written this book for the glory of God and to further His kingdom here on earth. I hope you enjoy this book and please share it with others as God leads you to do.

Evelyn Beelaert

CONTENTS

Dedication

Author's Preface

Chapter 1 - Prayer Alerts   Page

    1. Precious Cargo   4
    2. In the Water   6
    3. Night Watch   8
    4. Oh Andrew!   9
    5. Surprise Encounter   16
    6. What a Shock   18

Chapter 2 - Testimonies of Hope

    1. Valley of the Shadow   22
    2. My Goliath   27

Chapter 3 – God Moments
    1. God Our Protector   31
    2. God Gives Confirmation   33
    3. God Our Provider   36
    4. The Fleece   38
    5. New Friend   40
    6. Daily Guidance   41
    7. Prayers for our Needs   43
    8. Best God Moment of All   44

CHAPTER 1 - PRAYER ALERTS

PRECIOUS CARGO

The bus was noisy and crowded with teenagers heading home on I-65 from a week long retreat in Daytona Beach, Florida. The year was 1987, and my husband was driving the church bus. We were in a convoy of three large Greyhound size buses, and ours was the middle bus.

Before we left Florida, I remember praying for God to protect us and put his guardian angels around our bus, and to guide my husband's hands and feet at the controls. Since I myself am a mother, I knew how precious was our cargo of young people and how anxiously the parents were awaiting their safe arrival.

We stopped to eat dinner at Shoney's and soon were back on the road. The rhythm of the old bus' engine and tires soon had me almost asleep. I suddenly felt an urgent need to pray for the safety of the buses. As I was praying, I felt with a certainty that lives were in jeopardy. I started to ask the entire bus to pray but resisted the urge and continued praying. Fear was almost overwhelming me, so urgent was the need I felt to pray. After a while, I felt a peaceful assurance that my prayer had been heard. I continued praying off and on, thanking God for hearing my prayers.

The bus started bouncing and swaying and I heard the squeal of air-brakes and gravel spraying. Loose objects flew through the air as passengers clutched the seats to keep from falling. Soon I realized we were off the road and on the shoulder, within arms' reach of the bus ahead of us.

I remember the surge of fear during those few short moments of chaos until the bus stopped abruptly. My next thought was thankfulness to God for saving our precious cargo. I also knew at that moment, without any doubt, that this near disaster was the reason I was called to pray so urgently.

The lead bus had been forced to brake violently and go to the shoulder due to an accident happening immediately in front of it. Our bus and the one behind us had to react in the same way to avoid a multi-vehicle collision.

Our God is an awesome God. He not only answers our prayers but also tells us when to pray. He guides us to pray for specific needs, especially if those needs involve the safety and well-being of His children.

"For he will give his angels charge concerning you, to guard you in all your ways. They will bear you up in their hands, lest you strike your foot against a stone." Psalms 91:11-12

We were safe, not a single person on any of the three buses had been harmed in any way. As for me, my faith was strengthened and I have the honor of sharing this wonderful story of God's love and protection of his children.

If you think about it, God really didn't need me to pray the bus to safety. He could have spoken the word and it would have been done. Instead, he chose me as a prayer warrior that day. I felt honored and amazed at the power of prayer and the Holy Spirit. This was my very first prayer alert and I was overwhelmed by what had just happened. God was preparing me but I really didn't know that then. He is the potter, we are the clay.

IN THE WATER

In 1991, my first daughter, Lori, was six years old. She spent time before and after school and on some school holidays at a daycare called Fun Company. The YMCA sponsored Fun Company and Lori really enjoyed her time and her friends there.

One day after dropping Lori off at Fun Company, as I was driving to work on the interstate, I again felt the urgent need to pray. I asked the Lord to reveal to me who I should pray for and Lori's name came to my mind. Fear like a river poured into me and I started crying while I was driving. I knew with a certainty that Lori would be facing some unknown danger and that I had to pray for her immediately. I prayed over and over again for Lori's safety and protection as I drove to work that day in tears. After a while, the fear was replaced with a peace that my prayer had been heard and that Lori would be alright.

When I picked Lori up from Fun Company that afternoon, the first thing she said to me in her innocence was "Mommy, I drowned today." I asked her what she meant and she explained that her cousin, Carlye, was at the YMCA pool when Fun Company arrived on their swimming field trip. Carlye is eight years older than Lori and was born with Down's syndrome.

Carlye could swim very well but Lori was not yet a swimmer. Lori told me that her cousin had played with her in the pool and carried her out to the deep end and then just left her there. She did not do it intentionally; she just didn't realize that Lori had not yet learned to swim. Lori said that her head went under the water three times and somehow, after the third time, she made it to the side of the pool and pulled herself up from the water. None of the adults had seen it happen, but they helped her get out of the pool and calmed her down after the incident.

I know in my heart that God heard my prayers and saved my child from drowning that day. After all, she is His child, too, and just given to me as a gift to cherish and love.

"Behold, children are a gift of the Lord. The fruit of the womb is a reward." Psalms 127:3

Lori learned to swim and helped teach her baby sister, Rachel, to swim as well. Carlye later participated in the Special Olympics many times for swimming events and did very well.

Lori is 28 years old now with two babies of her own. I am thankful to God for every day of her 28 years and for my grandchildren. Life is so very precious. I am comforted knowing that the God of the universe also watches so very carefully after our children.

"Like a shepherd He will tend His flock. In His arms He will gather the lambs and carry them in His bosom; He will gently lead the nursing ewes." Isaiah 40:11 He is our good shepherd as he told us in John 10:11, "I am the good shepherd; the good shepherd lays down his life for the sheep."

Yes, He laid down his life for the sheep and now He lives again and watches His flock so very closely. In Psalms 121:3 we read "he will not allow your foot to slip; he who keeps you will not slumber. Behold, he who keeps Israel will neither slumber nor sleep."

Did God send an unseen angel to Lori that day after I prayed for her? I believe He did. I think an angel assisted her in getting safely to the side of the pool. To God be the glory now and forevermore. Thank you God!

Night Watch

Rachel was born in August of 1993 and, as all new babies do, kept me up off and on during the night. I was a nursing mother and enjoyed my nursing relationship with the baby. The night shift is what I jokingly called getting up to nurse the baby during the night.

It was during one of the night shifts in Rachel's first year that I again was called upon to pray for a loved one in danger. I sometimes used the quiet time I spent during the night while nursing to pray. During this prayer time, Carlye's name came to me for urgent prayer. I remember it was 2am when this happened as I checked the bedside clock. So urgent was the need to pray for Carlye that fear for her safety engulfed me. I started to call my sister, Thelma, her mother, but at 2am I was reluctant to use the phone. Instead, I continued to pray until I felt the peace that comes in knowing my prayer had been heard and she would be alright.

I called Thelma first thing the next morning and asked about Carlye. She said that the strangest thing had happened to Carlye during the night. She told me she had heard her choking during the night and rushed to her room to check on her. She assured me that Carlye was ok and that she was unsure of the cause of her choking episode. I asked her what time it had happened and she said around 2am. I shared with Thelma my prayers for Carlye during the night and that I almost called her to check on my niece around 2am.

God truly does not slumber or sleep and certainly proved it to me that night. He rescues us in need no matter what the hour. He will not forget us. "Can a woman forget her nursing child, and not have compassion on the son of her womb? Surely they may forget, yet I will not forget you." Isaiah 49:15

OH ANDREW!!

I love Sunday mornings. On this Sunday morning, I was sitting in my husband's office, folding laundry and trying to wake up to get ready for church. My husband was working at his computer. My cell phone rang and I immediately thought something was wrong when I saw my daughter Lori's name pop up on the display so very early on a Sunday morning.

Lori's voice was so full of panic and tears that I knew something terrible had happened. My heart started racing and my breath caught as I heard her say "Momma, a tree fell on Andrew!" I will never forget the pain and suffering in her voice, it makes me cry even now as I write this.

Lori and Andrew were newlyweds. They had only been married six weeks when I got this phone call. Andrew loves to hunt, and on the first day of hunting season, he and his best friend, Jeff, took off for a five day hunting trip to Land Between the Lakes in Kentucky. I asked Lori how she felt about Andrew leaving her for five days so soon after the wedding. She told me that she had to work all weekend at the hospital anyway, so the timing was good. She was a registered nurse at the UT Medical Center in Knoxville and worked every other weekend. I later found out that Andrew had indeed missed his new wife very badly while on his hunting trip. After only one day apart, Lori told me Andrew had called her and told her how much he wished he could hurry home to her. That was the night before the accident.

That Sunday morning before I got Lori's call, Andrew and Jeff were perched in separate tree stands hoping to see deer. Andrew was 30 feet up in his tree. Jeff saw a tree fall that morning toward the direction of Andrew's tree stand. Jeff immediately went to check on Andrew, fearing the worst. He found him unconscious and bleeding from his mouth lying against a tree. Jeff turned him over to keep him from choking on his own blood. He tried to get 911 on his cell phone but the cell signal did not reach that far back into the woods. Jeff knew it was a life and death situation to get Andrew medical help and ran as fast as he could through the woods toward the closest road, about two miles, trying his cell phone along the way. By the time he reached the road, help had arrived and Jeff led them back to Andrew. Andrew, the thought of you battered and broken lying there unconscious, bleeding and all alone breaks my heart.

The paramedics soon loaded him onto a Life Flight helicopter and transported him quickly to Vanderbilt University Hospital where trauma teams were waiting. In the helicopter the life flight nurse had to resuscitate Andrew and saved his life. Upon arrival in the trauma ICU, they first did a CT scan which found air pockets around his heart. This was making his heart struggle to pump and would damage his heart. They immediately took him for heart surgery and opened his chest. They found the tissues between the lungs and heart had ruptured on both sides. They repaired the tissues, closed him up and hoped for the best. It was determined he had facial fractures, skull fractures, collapsed lungs, broken ribs, damaged spleen and adrenal glands, his lower spine had burst and three of his back teeth were knocked out. Andrew was fighting for his life. His left eye was swollen to a size larger than a golf ball and the eye was horribly disfiguring. Oh Andrew! You are broken and suffering and we can't even talk to you.

They put Andrew under heavy sedation after the heart surgery. That is how he remained day after day. It was determined at one point a few days later that Andrew was stable enough to have surgery on his face. They put five plates in his face to piece it back together, particularly the area around his badly damaged left eye.

I was praying for Andrew but I did not feel the anointing from the Holy Spirit. If ever I needed help from God, this was the time! In desperation I prayed to God, trying to find out why the Holy Spirit was not active and helping me to pray. I asked God to reveal to me the reason that the Holy Spirit had left me and asked Him if it was sin on my part. Confirmation came quickly through the anointing that sin was blocking my prayers. I prayed for God to reveal what my sin was and He revealed that it was something I had watched on the internet. I immediately repented to God and promised Him I would never do it again. God sees our actions as well as our heart. The Holy Spirit can only live in a holy place. If sin is there, He will be grieved and can't help you in your prayers as He can't be with you.

God is so good. As soon as I truly repented and promised to turn away from my sin and never do it again, His Holy Spirit came back to me. He led me to fast and pray for Andrew. I had never fasted before and I did not think I could do it. However, seeing Andrew so battered and broken was unbearable and so was the thought of Lori living without him. I immediately did what God led me to do. When God calls you to fast, He will give you the strength you need to accomplish it. Your hunger pains are not as severe and He comforts you along the way. I did drink fluids. It says in God's Word when fasting to be of good countenance, not sad (Matthew 6:16-18). With His help, nobody knew I was fasting. My fast lasted for five days and during this time Andrew was unconscious and in intensive care. Lori and the rest of the family did not know if he would wake up and, if he did wake up, would he even know us? Was he paralyzed, would he walk again? The vigil at the hospital was round the clock and the rollercoaster ride of improvements then setbacks and more surgeries had begun.

I took Lori out to eat one day during this time. She was exhausted and needed to shower and eat. It is awkward when you are fasting if you go out to eat with someone. I remember just sipping the broth of the French onion soup and a glass of tea. Lori said something about me not eating and I did not reveal that I was fasting, just that I was satisfied. I think God blesses your fasting if you do not appear to others to be fasting. In fact, my countenance became more becoming the longer I fasted and my face and skin became radiant.

On the fifth day of fasting, Andrew was still lost to us. The longer he was gone from us, the more concerned we grew. However a verse came to me about fear. Fear is not from God; God gives you hope and comfort. I clung to this verse like a drowning man to a life vest. Psalms 23:4 "Yea, though I walk through the valley of the shadow of death, I will fear no evil: for thou art with me, thy rod and thy staff they comfort me." If God is with you, He replaces fear with hope and will comfort you as nobody else can. This especially happens when you know your prayers have reached His throne.

I was getting physically weak by the fifth day and did not know how much longer I would need to fast. I thought I should not eat until Andrew could eat again. That was human thinking, not God's plan.

While in the trauma intensive care waiting room, I felt the still small voice urging me to go to the chapel. I thought the chapel was on the eleventh floor but got to that floor and it was not there. God will send others to you if you lose your way when trying to do His bidding. A young man came to me and asked if he could help me and I said yes and asked where the chapel was located. He directed me to the first floor. I found the chapel and kneeled to pray at the altar prayer rail. The most beautiful music was being played by an individual in scrubs at the piano against the wall. I could tell she found peace and comfort there in God's place and was expressing herself and worshipping with the piano.

God knew what I was praying for and I felt His Holy Spirit well up within me in a mighty way. The living water was saturating my soul and soon I felt the prayer for Andrew physically leave my body. It was an amazing and wonderful feeling; my prayer was released like a hot-air balloon rising to God's throne. I had never experienced this before and was totally awed by the working of the Holy Spirit. For the first time in my life, after fasting for five days, I could feel His presence so strongly moving inside me that I had no doubt I was a new creature in Christ. It was amazing and comforting knowing that the God of all creation gave His Son and then sent His Holy Spirit to live inside me, a woman of no particular prestige or status. I did not earn it, you cannot buy it, and all you must do is believe that Jesus is "the Son of God who takes away the sin of the world." (John 1:29) Simply ask Him to forgive your sin and then sin no more so that the Holy Spirit will come live inside you. You will know He has come to you by the washing over you, the living water! The Holy Spirit must have a clean and holy vessel in which to dwell. You need the Holy Spirit in order for your prayers to reach our Father in Heaven. Sin can keep you from receiving the "Prayer Alerts" that the Holy Spirit sends to you when you need to pray for your family's protection. I had sinned and therefore was not alerted to pray for Andrew by the Holy Spirit. Oh Andrew, I am so very sorry. I did not get the "Prayer Alert" and did not know to pray for your protection.

I was not the only one praying for Andrew. At Vanderbilt Hospital they provided a "Caring Bridge" website for us to use to keep everyone up-to-date on Andrew's condition and it was overflowing with guestbook entries of people praying for Andrew. The love and support found there was very wonderful and helped the family greatly, especially during the darkest days.

After my visit to the chapel, I felt led to return home to Morristown, about 4 hours from Nashville. Spiritually, I was stronger than ever before in my life but physically I was weak. I was not sure when I should eat again and dared not break the fast until I was certain my job was done. I talked with my husband Jim as I drove the long way home that night. He told me that he had missed me very much and had baked an apple pie and had ice cream to serve with it waiting on me. First of all, I must confess that I am crazy about apple pie and vanilla ice cream! And the fact that my husband baked it was amazing indeed! He does not bake!!

I broke the fast and ate the best apple pie a 'la mode I had ever eaten. For several days afterwards my favorite foods kept appearing. God was spoiling me! Abba Father!

The next day after I returned home I rested and awaited news about Andrew. I had peace about Andrew ever since my prayer "balloon" had left me.

God is so good, He let me know when it was time to return to the hospital in Nashville for, at the very moment I got off on the tenth floor of the hospital, I heard weeping in the hospital hallway leading to Andrew's bed in the trauma ICU. My heart froze as I recognized the women weeping were Lori and Linda (Andrew's mom). Then with gladness I realized they were crying tears of joy. Andrew had finally awakened and knew them for the first time since the accident. I was there the very moment it happened! Thank you Lord, YOU ARE GOD!! Andrew was alive and restored to us. He knew us! And you enabled me to be there when it happened. Thank you God! How Great Thou Art!

The author in summer of 2008, a year before Andrew's accident.

SURPRISE ENCOUNTER

The bright sunlight was piercing to my eyes. It was coming in through the window and reflecting on the mirror beside my bed, then bouncing back and hitting my eyelids, waking me up. Usually I sleep late on the weekends. My first thought was, God are you wanting me to get up early? I remembered I had made my mind up the night before to get up early and do some walking to help me get in better shape. I assumed God was giving me the wake up call to get me out and walking. He had a bigger plan than that.

I thought I would take a right on 11E and walk to the Waffle House where I would reward myself with breakfast. However, when I got to the intersection, I felt led to turn left and walk toward McDonald's. It was a nice day and I was enjoying my walk and the scenery along the way.

About halfway to McDonald's I passed St. Patrick's Church and lo and behold, my prayer partner Liz was changing the words on the church's message board. I was so happy to see her and greeted her right away. She was just as happy as I that we ran into each other. When she finished with the message board, she said since we are together, why don't we go to the small chapel and pray together? Being prayer partners, we prayed together quite often. I said yes and off we went to the small chapel in the church.

Liz prayed first and then I prayed. While praying, the Lord put it on my heart to pray this prayer. "Dear God, we pray for whatever or whomever it is that you have called us here to pray for this morning." I have had many prayer alerts in my life and I thought perhaps this was more than a coincidence for us to meet that morning. Could this be because of divine providence? I prayed this prayer just in case there was something we should pray for that we were not aware of.

Liz and I parted soon after. I went to McDonald's for breakfast and then walked back home. My day was off to a great start!

A few hours later, I got a call from Liz. I could tell something had happened by the tone of her voice. She was shaken. Liz said, "I know what it was we were called to pray for this morning. My daughter-in-law, Amy, was just in a car accident shortly after we prayed this morning. If she hadn't looked up and checked her mirror, her car would have been totaled by a drunk driver." By looking up at the right moment, she was able to maneuver her car in such a way to lessen the impact. Amy told Liz that her guardian angel must have been watching over her for her to be able to see and react so quickly. Her car was badly damaged but Amy and her children were fine. I truly believe God did send an angel to protect her and her family, and that our combined prayers that morning set angels in motion. (Matthew 18:20 "For where two or three are gathered together in my name, I am there in the midst of them.")

I would like to say I kept on walking on a daily basis but truly I did not. When I did walk after that day, it was in the evenings. I am truly not a morning person, except for that one day that God woke me up with a ray of sunlight so bright it almost blinded me. He gave me the blessing of answered prayer that day and Liz the blessing of safety for her family. His ways are higher than ours, in Isaiah 55:8-9 we read "For my thoughts are not your thoughts, nor are your ways my ways," says the Lord. "For as the heavens are higher than the earth, so are my ways higher than your ways, and my thoughts than your thoughts." God will lead us where we need to be exactly when we need to be there. This enables us to do his work here on earth, even if it takes two or more! Amen and thank you God!

What a Shock!

It was just an ordinary day at work, a Tuesday. I had no lunch plans so I just got a can of chili from the vending machine to stave my hunger.

A thought kept coming to me to go to a Christian bookstore and find a music CD to help me pray. I usually don't go out at lunch but the urging I felt was from God and so I got in the car and off I went to a Christian bookstore near work.

I found a music CD called "Deeper" which said "2 hours of Deep Worship for Prayer and Intercession" and I purchased it. The lady at the checkout counter asked if she could pray with me after she checked me out and we did pray together right there at the checkout counter. She said she loved the chance to pray with her customers.

I got to my car and immediately inserted the first of the two CD's. The first song was "Welcome in This Place" and it was a song to the Holy Spirit telling Him that He is welcome inside you and asking Him to saturate your soul with His presence. I immediately felt Him with me in my car and the peace, joy and love that He brings is so wonderful. I listened to the music and prayed for His guidance. He put it on my heart to fast and pray for my husband, Jim. I thought it was for Jim's spiritual needs as Jim was still hurting from the death of his first wife the previous year from cancer.

I fasted and prayed for 24 hours and listened to the music CD a lot during that time. There was another song on it called "Revelation Song" on which I felt the Holy Spirit's strong anointing. The words of the song come straight from the book of Revelation. Rev. 4:8 reads "Holy, holy, holy, Lord God Almighty, which was and is, and is to come."

I have found that when God lays it on your heart to fast and pray, He gives you the strength to do it. Also, as your body gets weaker, your spirit gets stronger, which is why, if it is a desperate need, He places it on your heart to fast as well as pray. If you are spiritually strong, your prayers are more powerful.

By dinnertime the next day, I had the peace that comes from the Holy Spirit assuring me my prayers had been heard and I could end the fast. God is so good, He seems to provide you with your favorite foods at the end of each fast as if to say well done, this food is for you to enjoy now.

On Friday, I called my husband Jim to check on him. I rarely called him due to his busy schedule as a general contractor. He sounded very "shook up" and said that everyone was saying he had "someone watching over him."

He had been working on an electrical wiring problem and had accidently crossed two 270 volt wires (very high current). When the wires crossed it killed all the power to eight entire floors of the bank building where he was working.

Jim's confidence was shaken and he said that he was considering not doing the "hands on" work anymore. When the wires crossed, he could have electrocuted all of his men as well as himself. I knew it must have been a close call or he would not have been so upset. The power from the crossed wires went into the ceiling which kept him and his men from being injured. Was the "someone watching over him" his guardian angel?

I thought I was praying for a spiritual concern for Jim, but as it turned out it was a physical safety issue for him and his men. God knows everything, our thoughts, our needs and our future, as well as the future of our family members. He is faithful to watch over his children like a shepherd. As David said in Psalm 23, "The Lord is my shepherd; I shall not want." We don't have to want because he will provide for our needs and our safety as well, and for the safety of our family (our precious flock of loved ones). AMEN!

This original painting of Jesus was done by the author in 2013 with inspiration from a painting by Cale Bramer.

Postscript

This is by no means the end of the Prayer Alerts stories. I will continue to journal them as they happen and will follow God's still small voice to write what He leads me to share.

I have asked God to give me prayer alerts for our nation as well. Only God can deliver us from evil and heal our land. To date I have had only one prayer alert for our nation.

God bless and keep you always. If you have not accepted Jesus yet, he is waiting for you to open the door and let Him into your heart. He is God's son, He died for you, His blood washes away all your sins so that God can see you and answer your prayers. He rose from the dead and is seated at the right hand of God the Father on the Mercy Seat. Ask God to forgive your sins and accept Jesus as your Savior. He will put a new spirit within you, the Holy Spirit, and will also give you eternal life. I hope to see you in eternity.

Praise His Holy Name!

Evelyn Beelaert

Chapter 2 - Testimonies of Hope

A Letter to the Homeless – Fall 2013

Valley of the Shadow

Dear Friend,
I really had no intention of going to the mall that day. I was out running errands all by myself. Mall time is more fun with a friend or with family. By the third time the thought came to my mind about going to the mall, I knew it had to be God speaking to me. That is how he works. I really didn't have anything I needed to buy and money was tight, plus going to the mall by myself seemed awkward, but off to the mall I went.

I parked in my usual parking space, outside the corner entrance of Belk. I always park in the same area so I don't have to search for my car later in the huge parking lot. God knows our habits, and he certainly knew mine. When I entered the mall, the first thing I saw was a big banner about breast cancer. It was in the lobby right above the store entrance. When I read how many thousands of people die of breast cancer each year, my heart was moved with compassion for all the victims and their families and friends. The banner was urging us to help in the fight against breast cancer.

Immediately I thought to pray to God about breast cancer. I know our God can do anything and has told us we just need to ask Him. I prayed "Dear God, I pray for a cure for breast cancer" and then added as an afterthought "in my lifetime". I immediately felt the anointing from the Holy Spirit very strongly giving me confirmation that God had heard my prayer and would answer it.

Joy in abundance flooded my soul and I wanted to share with everyone what God had just revealed to me. He was going to cure breast cancer in my lifetime! I thanked Him and praised His holy name right there under the banner. I knew people would not believe me if I told them and perhaps think I was crazy, so I decided to keep my knowledge to myself and just wait and watch for God to work to cure breast cancer.

I went in the mall afterward but was not even interested in shopping. I left soon after and knew that my purpose at the mall was to see the banner and pray. I was very surprised at how strong the anointing was when God answered. It was unmistakable.

About three weeks after my trip to the mall I went for my annual mammogram. They called me the next day and asked me to do another one as they wanted to get a better view. I went back the very next day and the radiologist called me back to her office and showed me the area of concern. She said she wanted to needle biopsy it as soon as possible. At this point I was not really too worried as I had had a needle biopsy once before. The biopsy appointment was made and after the biopsy they sent the specimen to the lab and said they would call me when they got the results.

The radiologist called me three days later. I could tell from her voice it wasn't good news. She told me I had ductal carcinoma in situ which means it was in the milk duct. I was shocked and my first reaction was fear for my life and also a profound sadness at the thought of leaving my family to go on without me. Our family was recently blessed with two grandbabies that I planned on watching grow up. The thought of not being there for them was devastating.

Then God stepped in. He immediately brought to my mind memories of the strong anointing He gave me when I prayed for a cure for breast cancer in my lifetime. I knew then why the anointing was so strong. *God was preparing me for this day. I realized He had promised to cure me before I even knew I had breast cancer!*

Peace like a river came to me and I was no longer afraid. *We truly are more than conquerors in Christ. Romans 8:37 "Yet in all these things we are more than conquerors through Him who loved us." A conqueror does not know beforehand if he will win the fight. God had already revealed to me the outcome of my breast cancer! I knew as soon as I was given the diagnosis that I would survive.* How amazing is his love for us. The Bible says he knows the number of hairs on our head. Matthew 10:30 "And even the very hairs of your head are all numbered". In addition to hair, I know now that he also knows *every cell in our body* as well. His love is so great it is hard to describe. He watches over us lovingly and will never forsake us.

I know some of the nurses and doctors at the hospital may have thought I was strange. I had to have two surgeries and both times I was happy and smiling and not the least bit scared. Then it came time for my 16 radiation treatments (double doses each time). They gave me the lifetime maximum radiation that I can have in that part of my body.

I had fun and kidded around with the technicians doing the radiation treatments. They told me I was the happiest cancer patient they had ever seen. They would give me extra spins on the table and we would laugh. They looked forward to seeing me every morning and I them.

Before the last treatment, I broke some glow sticks and put them under my gown on my chest. When they came in I told them I thought they had given me too much radiation and pointed to my glowing chest. We laughed again. I then told them this story on the day of my last treatment. It moved them greatly.

Psalm 23:4 "Yeah though I walk through the Valley of the Shadow of death, I will fear no evil, for thou art with me, thy rod and thy staff, they comfort me" is one of my favorite psalms that King David wrote so many years ago. I was in that valley of the shadow and God was with me. He gave me joy and peace instead of fear. He will do the same for you if you will receive Him. These are the simple steps.

- Believe Jesus is God's only son, conceived by the Holy Spirit and born of the virgin Mary, believe he was crucified, died and was buried and that on the third day he rose again. He lives again and sits on the right hand of God the Father and will come again to judge the quick (living) and the dead.
- Ask God to forgive your sins and promise to turn away from them. Ask him to reveal your sins to you, known and unknown and turn away from them.
- Ask Jesus to come into your heart and make you a new creation, ready to be filled with the Holy Spirit and live for eternity with God.

The Holy Spirit has to have a clean home in order to dwell inside you, and He will comfort and guide you like He did me. He led me to that banner where He gave me the promise of healing when I prayed. Note that I was praying for others and it turned out that God blessed me as well.

Jesus's precious blood is the only cleanser that can clean us completely so that the Holy Spirit will come to live inside us. Not good works, not good intentions, only Jesus' blood will prepare the way for the Holy Spirit to descend on you and dwell within you. The fruits of having the spirit live inside you are love, joy, peace, patience, kindness, goodness, faithfulness, gentleness and self-control (Galatians 5:22-23)

If you haven't accepted Jesus yet, don't wait. Tomorrow is not promised to anyone. Pray this prayer: Dear God, I believe Jesus is your only son and he died on the cross for me and rose from the dead. Please forgive me for all my sins and I turn away from sin. Please wash me with Jesus' blood and fill me with the Holy Spirit so that I may have eternal life with you. In Jesus' name, Amen.
(Lost Sheep Ministries Prayer Team – Evelyn)

Postscript
After the writing of this story, I spoke with Maxine, the founder of Lost Sheep Ministries, about my breast cancer healing experience and gave her a copy of my story. She shared with me that God would now be able to use me to heal others of breast cancer with the power of the Holy Spirit. She told me that she herself had been homeless at one time and that God had gotten her out of that life and then enabled her to start this ministry to help other homeless people. In other words, what God delivers you from, He will enable you to deliver others from it as well through the working of the Holy Spirit.

Maxine was right. God has brought to my attention at least three women for healing of breast cancer since that time. I have had the honor to pray for them and have felt that same strong anointing that I had when He promised to heal me. Some were in advanced stages of breast cancer. God did answer my prayer for a cure for breast cancer in my lifetime. The cure is faith in Him. Amen

A Letter to the Homeless –2012
My Goliath

Dear Friend,

I have a true story to share with you. God gave me this story and He asked me to share it with you as He loves you so very much.

One day my new son-in-law, Andrew, was injured and near death due to a fall from a tree stand while deer hunting. He was about thirty feet off the ground when a falling tree hit his tree and knocked him from his position. His life was in serious jeopardy and it was truly a miracle that he even made it to the hospital alive. Rescue workers put him on a life flight helicopter and he was resuscitated several times before he finally reached the hospital. He had emergency surgery to remove the air and fluid from around his heart because his lungs had collapsed. The air from his lungs was pressing on his heart. This was the first surgery. Next he had five plates put in his face and one eye was in jeopardy of being lost forever, his spine was burst and many ribs broken and the injury list went on and on.

I prayed for Andrew and my prayers were not being heard. I asked God if sin was blocking my prayers. Imagine my shame when God confirmed that yes, sin was blocking my prayers! Immediately I asked God to forgive my sins and hear my prayers for Andrew. I'm sharing this with you so you will know that sin will block your prayers. As soon as I repented and asked forgiveness, God heard me and started answering my prayers for Andrew! Andrew came out of his coma and God restored his life. After many surgeries and much suffering, Andrew is now a walking miracle!

The next big trial I faced was two years later when my husband rejected me and asked me to leave our home. I was devastated and turned to God for help and comfort. God revealed to me that Andrew was my "lion and my bear" and that my husband's rejection was my "Goliath".

If you remember the Bible story of David and Goliath, you may recall that it was while David was tending his father's sheep that he had to kill a lion and a bear with his bare hands in order to protect them. His triumph over these predators prepared David and also convinced the king to let David fight against the giant Philistine, Goliath, who was over nine feet tall. As you probably know from the Bible story, David declined to wear the king's armor for protection and killed Goliath while carrying only a shepherd's staff and using a slingshot and a stone (I Samuel 17:33 -50).

One day, when at lunch with my friends, I mentioned that Andrew had been my "lion and my bear" and that my husband was my "Goliath". Immediately, my friend Kathy spoke up and said "you are right!" I asked her what she meant and she said that God had given both me and David a Goliath to face. This surely meant that one day all of us would have to face a Goliath at some point in our lives.

A week or so later, Kathy was diagnosed with stage four pancreatic cancer and given three to six months to live without treatment. Her Goliath had come and he was every bit as huge, deadly and menacing as David's uncircumcised Philistine had been all those many years ago (I Samuel 17:36). Last week Kathy had her first chemo treatment. I asked her that morning if I could go with her and carry her "bag of stones" as she went forth to fight Goliath. Kathy has a very strong faith and replied "no, I only need one stone".

After that statement, she immediately remembered a beautiful shiny black stone her friend David had given her just a few days before. He said he had kept the stone for a long time and that he now wanted Kathy to have his "special" stone.

When Kathy's friend, Lil, came to pick her up for her first chemo treatment a short time later, Kathy told Lil that the cancer was her Goliath and then mentioned that I had offered to go with her and carry her bag of stones that morning. Kathy also mentioned the pretty black stone that David had given her recently.

Lil immediately jumped to her feet and rushed to the door, telling Kathy she needed to get something from the car and would be right back.

When Lil returned, in her hand she held a small stone with the name "GOD" on it. She told Kathy that it had been in her purse for five years and that God had told her to give it to Kathy that very morning. She had planned to wait until they got to the hospital to do so. Lil's eyes were streaming with tears when she gave Kathy the "GOD" stone. Five years before, Lil had taught a Bible study about the fact that God is our rock (Matthew 7:24 – 27). To reinforce the lesson, Lil had passed out the "GOD" stones and had been carrying hers in her purse ever since.

Please accept this "GOD" stone today as assurance that God will be with you when you fight your own Goliath. He confirmed His presence for Kathy with a stone just like this as she faces her Goliath. This stone will also remind you of a small handsome shepherd boy, David, who used just one small stone to save his people from a fierce and deadly enemy.

You may be fighting your own Goliath right now. Please know that in order for God to be with you and hear your prayers, you must ask for forgiveness of your sins just as I did. You only need to ask and Jesus will be your Savior. He is waiting patiently. All you have to do is believe in Him.

I hope this story will help you to believe in Christ. Believe that He is God's son, that He died on the cross for us and that He rose from the grave on the third day. His blood washes away all our sins so that God can see us and hear our prayers. He will fight our Goliaths with us and also give us eternal life. He sits at the right hand of God the Father in the Mercy Seat and will give you his Holy Spirit as soon as you believe. The Holy Spirit will lead, guide and protect you and also help you pray as you fulfill God's purpose for your life.

As a child of the living God, you don't have to face the lion, the bear and Goliath all on your own. I pray we will see each other for eternity. May God bless and protect you until then! (Lost Sheep Ministries Prayer Team – Evelyn)

A picture of Kathy's hand holding the rock her friend David had given her and also the God rock from Lil.

A picture of a God rock the author paints to give to the homeless along with this Goliath story.

CHAPTER 3 - GOD MOMENTS

GOD OUR PROTECTOR

Looking out the window I could hardly believe a drug deal was going on right before my eyes. A friend at my office said she could see drug deals going on from the third floor windows, a floor above my office.

She was right; they met on the corner across from our building, thinking nobody was watching. How long had this been going on? Our office is located in the heart of homeless territory, near the rescue mission. Drugs and alcohol are keeping the homeless trapped in a prison of their own making. I know God can set these prisoners free!

Gazing out the window, I prayed for God to stop the drug dealing right outside our office window. I prayed this evil be stopped to His glory. I knew my prayer had been heard with confirmation from the Holy Spirit.

After turning this problem over to Him, I continued my daily routine at work.

One day, a few weeks later, I was at my desk on the second floor and I heard footsteps coming toward me. I looked up and saw the building facility manager accompanied by four men, three of them in police uniforms. I thought to myself, what have I done wrong? Did I run a red light?

The facility manager explained that he wanted to introduce me to the officers, one of which was under cover. He explained they would be coming and going in our office building. They were investigating drug activity outside our building.

Immediately I remembered having prayed while looking out the third floor windows for God to stop the drug dealing and remembered the confirmation I had gotten that day that God had heard my prayer. Seeing these five men at my desk convinced me that indeed my prayer had been heard.

I told the officers that I was the reason they were there. I explained I had prayed to God for the drug dealing to be stopped and that I could show them an observation point on the third floor where they could see the drug activity. In the back of my mind I wondered if these men were angels in disguise.

They explained that they had just left the third floor. I asked if they knew about Chester (name changed), the biggest drug dealer out there? I had prayed with Chester several times at the lost sheep meetings for the homeless. I had prayed that God would turn Chester's life around and that he would become God's man and lead other homeless to Christ.

The officers told me that Chester had been arrested and was in jail. The clean-up had begun! Sometimes you have to hit rock bottom before you look up for salvation, I hoped that this was true for Chester.

I prayed for the safety of the drug enforcement officers in our building and for God to help them in their task. I smile as I write this knowing God answered my prayer and also let me meet the men he sent to answer them. What a wonderful and mighty God we serve!

GOD GIVES CONFIRMATION

Bam, the car jolted and my head flew forward then back. I was sitting stopped at a red light and had just been rear-ended.

I got out and spoke to the other driver and viewed the damage. The other driver was a young girl that admitted she was looking at her cell phone when she hit me. She was a very sweet young lady and I felt sorry for her. She didn't have proof of insurance and the police officer gave her a citation.

I went home and hoped that she really did have insurance so I could get my car repaired. I also had another concern on my mind. I bought reading glasses for the homeless every week and passed them out at the prayer table at Lost Sheep Ministries meetings each Wednesday night. The meetings had been crowded and many reading glasses were being given out. I was concerned that perhaps the glasses were not the items on which God would have me spend my funds. Perhaps I should be purchasing other items for the homeless? Was I spending too much? Could I continue to fund this increasing need on my own? I prayed to God about it and asked for direction and confirmation that I was doing His will by buying and giving out the reading glasses.

A few weeks later, I dropped my car off at the auto repair shop. I showed them the damage on my back bumper. I also showed them the damage on my side view mirror. I had damaged it and had to replace the cover, which needed to be painted. They gave me a quote on the cost and I advised them to go ahead and repair both areas.

Before getting my car back from the repair shop, my back went out! I couldn't go to work and was on pain medication at home.

The auto repair shop called and said my car was ready. I advised them I was not able to drive because of pain medications and they offered to bring the car to my home. I accepted the kind offer and soon they arrived.

My car was perfect, more new looking than it had been in a long time. They detailed it and even vacuumed it. I was impressed with the work that had been done.

I asked how much I owed for fixing the mirror and the owner of the company advised two hundred and fifty dollars. I wrote him a check and hoped my checking account would last until next payday!

I asked if he would look at my daughter's car to make some body repairs to it. He came in the garage and looked it over, but the cost was way above my ability to pay.

After examining my daughter's car, he looked around my garage. He noticed a big blue basket on the floor and asked what the basket was for.

I picked up items from the basket and showed him the reading glasses for the homeless and explained they needed them to read the Bibles we pass out at the Lost Sheep Ministries meetings under the bridge. He asked me if I purchased them myself and I said yes. He proceeded to tell me what a blessed life he had. He had much more than he needed.

He tore up the check I had just given him and advised that he would not take any money from me and for me to keep helping the homeless. I was almost speechless. I thanked him and knew at that moment I was doing what God wanted me to do. This was my confirmation.

I was able to buy two hundred and fifty pairs of reading glasses thanks to his generosity. I knew now that not only did God want me to purchase the glasses; he would provide a way to do so.

I am still buying reading glasses for the homeless and now have no doubt this is important in God's eyes. Confirmation came through a small dent in my car and a kind man with a big heart (perhaps one of God's angels?).

I pray the homeless will use these glasses to read this story so they will know how precious they are in His sight. Copies of this book will be given to the homeless along with reading glasses and God's love.

A picture of the homeless at Lost Sheep Ministries Thanksgiving dinner under the interstate bridge, Knoxville, Tennessee, November 14, 2012.

God Our Provider

When I went to the garage to do my weekly mowing, I discovered that my lawn tractor would not start. I needed help, so I contacted my neighbor, Jim. Jim helped me remove the battery and advised me I should go to the auto store and have it tested. I left for the auto store with the battery. On the way out of my subdivision, I noticed a garage sale sign to my left down in a cul-de-sac. I regretfully went on by without stopping since I was on a mission to fix my lawn mower.

I soon arrived at the auto store and had the battery tested and replaced with a new one. On the way back home, I saw the garage sale again. I was thinking the mower was soon to be fixed so why not stop a moment at the garage sale?

I mentioned to the homeowner that if they had anything to donate after the garage sale was over, to give me a call and I would come and pick it up and take it to Lost Sheep Ministries for the homeless. A gentleman sitting next to her spoke up asking if I could use men's clothes for the homeless. I got really excited then because we have less donations for men than women. I guess men don't clean out their closets as often as women do!

I told him yes, men's clothes are greatly needed. He said he had three large trash bags full that he was going to give to Goodwill and would I take them instead? I said yes, of course, and he went to his home across the street to get the clothes and then proceeded to fill my trunk completely up with men's clothes. I thanked him for his generous gift and prayed blessings on him for his kindness. I left the clothes in my trunk as I did not get a chance to take them to the Lost Sheep Ministries warehouse. When Wednesday night came, I decided to deliver the men's clothes directly to the men's table for distribution to the homeless. We normally take them to the warehouse first for preparation.

When I arrived at the weekly Lost Sheep Ministries meeting for the homeless, I signed in on the volunteer sheet and then went to the prayer table where I volunteer. I remembered the clothes that were completely filling up the trunk of my car and mentioned to Sam, the leader of the prayer table, that I needed help getting the trunk full of men's clothes to the men's distribution table. Sam immediately asked if I had gotten the memo about the ministry being completely out of men's clothes. I told him no, I did not. I told him that apparently I did not need a memo; God led me to the clothes!

Sam and I took the clothes to the waiting homeless men that were standing in line. There was nothing on the tables to give them. God provided the clothes that day, using me, a broken lawnmower trip and a neighbor's garage sale to do so. In Matthew 25:35-40 we read "For I was hungry, and you fed me. I was thirsty, and you gave me drink. I was a stranger, and you invited me into your home. I was naked, and you gave me clothing. I was sick, and you cared for me. I was in prison, and you visited me. Then these righteous ones will reply, Lord, when did we ever see you hungry and feed you? Or thirsty and give you something to drink? Or a stranger and show you hospitality? Or naked and gave you clothing? When did we ever see you sick or in prison and visit you?" And the King will say, "I tell you the truth, when you did it to one of the least of these my brothers and sister, you were doing it to me!"

God will help us as we minister to others. He will provide for others through us. We are his hands and his feet here on earth and he makes a way when there seems to be no way. Thank you, God!

The Fleece

One day at work my good friend Tina and I discussed forming a prayer group on our lunch hour once a week. We had another Christian friend, Debra, who was also interested in joining us for prayer. We first had to decide where to go that would be private and preferably off company premises and close to the office. We also needed a prayer group leader who would prepare for the meetings and hold a brief Bible study before we started our prayer time.

Tina had been given a vision of praying hands years before. I think the Lord was preparing her for the prayer ministry. I prayed that the Lord would appoint a leader for our prayer group and that He would let us know who it should be. The next morning while pouring myself a cup of coffee at the group coffee pot, the thought came to me to tell Tina that she should be the leader of the prayer group. It came to me out of the blue because I wasn't even thinking about our prayer group at the time. I also felt the anointing from God that this was from Him. I could hardly wait to tell Tina. I went to Tina's desk and she wasn't there so I went back to work at my desk. A little later the thought came to me again and I went to find Tina. I found her at her desk and immediately told her that I thought she should be the one to lead the prayer group.

Tina had the funniest look on her face and could hardly speak. I was afraid I had offended her in some way. I mentioned the prayer vision she had been given years before and that I thought this was her ministry.

I left Tina's desk thinking I had offended her. I was puzzled and concerned. A little while later Tina came to my desk and explained to me why she had been so speechless at my news. Tina had prayed the night before that if she was supposed to be the leader of the prayer group the Lord would have me to come to her and tell her so the very next day. This is exactly what I did. Tina was overwhelmed that the Lord had chosen her to lead the prayer group. She also was in awe that He used me to confirm her leadership as she had specifically requested in her prayers. She said she had laid out a "fleece." I wasn't sure what she meant and then when she explained it, I remembered the Bible story of Gideon and the fleece.

So Gideon said to God, "If you will save Israel by my hand as you have said – look, I shall put a fleece of wool on the threshing floor; if there is dew on the fleece only, and it is dry on all the ground, then I shall know that you will save Israel by my hand, as you have said." And it was so. When he rose early the next morning and squeezed the fleece together, he wrung the dew out of the fleece, a bowlful of water. Judges 6: 36-38

I'm sure Gideon and Tina felt the same astonishment when their prayers were answered so exactly. Tina was wise to ask for God's guidance in the same way Gideon did. God does not change. He is the same now as when He answered Gideon's prayer. I'm also sure that Gideon and Tina were a little frightened at what God had for them to do. In fact, Gideon laid out a second fleece, a reverse of the first one; to be sure that God was speaking to him through the fleece.

Our prayer group met on Wednesday's at a church nearby. Two more co-workers soon joined the group. We had wonderful Christian fellowship and spent time in study, worship and prayer. Tina was confident in her leadership and the group was blessed with answered prayers.

In Matthew 18:20 we read "For where two or three are gathered together in my name, I am there in the midst of them." He truly was in our midst at our small prayer group. I am also happy that he used me to answer Tina's prayer for guidance. Now, when I am unsure of what the Lord would have me do, I will lay out a fleece of my own. After all, he never changes.

"For I am the Lord, I do not change; therefore you are not consumed, O sons of Jacob." Malachi 3:6

NEW FRIEND

My good friend, Lee, and I met as a direct answer to prayer. I had a vacancy in my group and I prayed for a Christian to fill it. Unknown to me, Lee was praying for a job in my area, which would be closer to her home. God answered both our prayers at the same time. Lee came to work in my office and soon joined our prayer group and we worked together for a long time.

The Lord encourages us to ask him for his help. In Matthew 7:7 -8 we read "Ask, and it will be given you; seek, and you will find; knock, and it will be opened to you. For everyone who asks, receives, and he who seeks finds, and to him who knocks it will be opened." Verse 11 goes on to say "If you then, being evil, know how to give good gifts to your children, how much more will your Father who is in heaven give good things to those who ask him!"

Daily Guidance

On days I remember to ask the Lord for guidance first thing before I go to work, everything goes much better. To me, this is part of the "daily bread" Jesus said we should pray for.

I ask the Lord to solve my problems before they come to me. At first I felt guilty about asking Him to do that for me, but then when I think about how intelligent I am compared to how intelligent He is it only makes sense to ask for His help.

He has answered this prayer for me so many times and I am in awe of each God moment that resulted. Someone would call me with a piece of information and then the very next call will be someone with a problem that the previous caller's information is all I needed to solve the problem. In Jeremiah 32:27 we read "Behold, I am the Lord, the God of all flesh. Is there anything too hard for me?"

I also ask the Lord daily before I go to work to help me guard my mouth and that everything I say and do will glorify Him. David did the same thing. In Psalm 19:14 we read "Let the words of my mouth and the meditation of my heart be acceptable in your sight, O Lord, my strength and my Redeemer." In this same Psalm we read in Verse 7 that "The law of the Lord is perfect, converting the soul; the testimony of the Lord is sure, making wise the simple." David knew that the Lord can transform anyone, no matter how simple, into a wise person. David himself was a simple shepherd boy looking over his father's flock when God chose him to be king of all Israel. He was chosen because of his pure and simple heart.
I Samuel 16:7 talks about one of David's brothers who

was rejected for the position. "The Lord said to Samuel, "Do not look at his appearance or at his physical stature, because I have refused him. For the Lord does not see as man sees; for man looks at the outward appearance, but the Lord looks at the heart."

No wonder Jesus said "Suffer the little children to come unto me and forbid them not; for of such is the kingdom of heaven" Matthew 19:14 Jesus could see their pure and simple little hearts, hearts that are quick to forgive and forget, and to comfort others in need. Have you ever noticed how quickly a small child will try to comfort someone they know is upset? My daughter Rachel, when she was just seventeen months old would do this. If she caught me or her sister crying, even if we were pretending, she would come to us and pat us and hug us. She stopped playing and waited until we were all "better" before she would leave us and resume her play.

God also knows the desires of our hearts. One of my favorite verses in the Bible is Psalm 37:4 "Delight yourself also in the Lord, and he shall give you the desires of your heart." Isn't that wonderful? He knows what we really want and will give it to us if we delight ourselves in Him. How do we do that? I think it is by praising and worshipping Him, by reading His Word, obeying Him, and communicating with Him through prayer.

In Psalm 32:7-8 David writes "You are my hiding place; you shall preserve me from trouble; you shall surround me with songs of deliverance. Selah I will instruct you and teach you in the way you should go; I will guide you with my eye." David knew God was not only our protector, but also our guide. At first this verse seemed odd to me that He would not guide us with His hand. I think that when he says He will guide us with His eye, He is telling us He sees where we are now and what is ahead. He is not a blind guide. He will lead us in safety to where we need to go. All we have to do is trust Him. Proverbs 3:5 tells us "Trust in the Lord with all your heart, and lean not on your own understanding; in all your ways acknowledge Him, and he shall direct your paths."

PRAYERS FOR OUR NEEDS

The Lord knows what we need and fills those needs, sometimes even before we ask Him. He has plans for us. In Philippians 1:6 we read what the apostle Paul wrote while he was in prison "being confident of this very thing, that he who has begun a good work in you will complete it until the day of Jesus Christ"... What confidence Paul had in Jesus that he could pen messages from his prison cell! He knew, as we too can know with certainty, God is in control of our lives and will finish what he starts in us until we accomplish his purpose for our lives. He will provide for all our needs in order to do this, sometimes even before we ask. God hears our every thought so we have no need to make a list for him as children do for Santa. So many times in my life I have wished for something and kept it to myself, thinking it not worthy of asking him for in prayer.

One day I was at Walmart and I started to purchase a pack of ink pens for work. I stopped and prayed for them instead and trusted God to provide them. The very next day my friend Teresa brought a whole new box of ink pens to my desk and I had not asked her to order them for me. Teresa said she thought I could use some new ink pens and left the whole box! Teresa is a Christian too and her husband does missionary work in Africa.

My prayer was answered that day by a Godly woman, but more importantly, I got a great big hug from the creator of the universe and a very special God moment. He once again proved his love for me by his concern for even my smallest needs. "And my God will supply all your needs according to His riches in glory in Christ Jesus" (Philippians 4:19).

BEST GOD MOMENT OF ALL

I had completed my morning routine and was in the car heading to work. I love playing songs of praise and worship as I drive and I can't help but sing along. God tells us to enter our closet and lock our door when we pray (Matthew 6:6). My car is one of my closets.

Mentally going over my plans for the day, I remembered that my daughter Lori, had asked me to come to dinner that night at their house. I had been praying for her and Andrew fervently as they were struggling in one area of their married life. They could not conceive a child. They were going to a fertility doctor for evaluation and help. Their worst fears were realized when they were told that Andrew was no longer able to father a child due to the life threatening accident he suffered the first year of their marriage. The situation looked grim as the doctor was unsure if Andrew would ever be healed of the injury and father a child.

Being a Christian means looking past what is possible with man, and praying for what is possible with God. In Matthew 19:26 we read "but Jesus beheld them, and said unto them, With men this is impossible; but with God all things are possible."

As I thought about dinner that night, it seemed odd to me that they had invited me on a weekday. Usually weekends were preferred times for family gatherings. The more I thought about it, the stranger and more out of the ordinary it seemed. I always try to figure things out. Andrew was infertile but I had prayed and gotten confirmation from the Holy Spirit that he would be healed. Now I was waiting for physical proof of the healing that God had revealed to me would happen. Could it be that Lori was expecting a baby? I prayed and asked God if this was why they had invited me to dinner. Confirmation from the Holy Spirit was strong and unmistakable.

My joy and thankfulness at that moment was more than I can put in words and tears rolled down my cheeks. I thanked and praised God and could not stop smiling knowing I was going to have a grandbaby! Praise His Holy Name!

I arrived at Lori's house thinking they would announce the pregnancy at the dinner table. I took my time eating my spaghetti but they were rushing through and even removed their plates and left me to finish at the table alone, so hurried they were! Doubt tried to creep in that perhaps I had misinterpreted what God had revealed to me that morning. Disappointed, I got up from the table and sat on the couch to talk to them after dinner.

Lori got up saying she needed to go to the bathroom. Soon she called Andrew into the bathroom with her, which I thought was strange indeed. Lori returned to the living room and broke the big news, she was pregnant! She had gone to the bathroom to get the pregnancy test as she was planning on showing me the test results. The results had faded so she had to tell me verbally. My prayers for them had been answered and God was blessing our family with new life. I blurted out that I knew already, that God had revealed it to me that very morning. I know they thought I was delusional.

In Psalm 139:13 we read "for you formed my inward parts; you knitted me together in my mother's womb." Yes, God had formed new life inside of Lori and had given them back joy and new hope for their future.
They knew life could end at any moment after Andrew's close brush with death and wanted a baby before anything else could happen to stop it. They treasured every day of life with each other with an appreciation of life that only those who have experienced near death can have.

My grandson is now two years old and more precious than words can say. God surprised us last year with another baby, this time a girl who arrived as our Christmas gift on December 20th and was home in time for Christmas. God is love, God is good, God reigns! Thank you God for your best gifts of all, children!
God has told us this in his word. In Matthew 19:14 we read "But Jesus said, Suffer little children, and forbid them not, to come unto me: for of such is the kingdom of heaven." He also says in Matthew 18:10 "Take heed that ye despise not one of these little ones; for I say unto you, that in heaven their angels do always behold the face of my Father which is in heaven."

I like to think the angels are there before God's face so that if any angel is needed urgently to protect the child that God has given them to guard, they are right there at His throne waiting for the command for them to act. God's love is ever watchful over his children, even more than human parents can be. God knows what is coming before it happens. All children are His, they have pure hearts and have not sinned against Him. This is my prayer for my heart to be as pure as a child that I may see His face when he calls me home. Matthew 5:8 "Blessed are the pure in heart: for they shall see God."

Peace and blessings to those who read this book. I pray I will see you in eternity with the one who gave His life for us, Jesus Christ! Jesus I am so in love with you!

Evelyn Beelaert

A picture of Jesus sketched in 2011 by the author with inspiration taken from a painting by Akiane Kramarik.

Made in the USA
Columbia, SC
25 January 2024